CRISISP

Why
Better Than Mine?

by Judith Couchman

A MINISTRY OF THE NAVIGATORS
P.O. BOX 35001, COLORADO SPRINGS, COLORADO 80935

The Navigators is an international Christian organization. Jesus Christ gave His followers the Great Commission to go and make disciples (Matthew 28:19). The aim of The Navigators is to help fulfill that commission by multiplying laborers for Christ in every nation.

NavPress is the publishing ministry of The Navigators. NavPress publications are tools to help Christians grow. Although publications alone cannot make disciples or change lives, they can help believers learn biblical discipleship, and apply what they learn to their lives and ministries.

Cover illustration by Catherine Kanner.

CRISISPOINTS FOR WOMEN series edited by Judith Couchman.

This series offers God's hope and healing for life's challenges.

All Scripture quotations in this publication are from the *Holy Bible: New International Version* (NIV). Copyright © 1973, 1978, 1984, International Bible Society. Used by permission of Zondervan Bible Publishers.

Printed in the United States of America

FOR A FREE CATALOG OF
NAVPRESS BOOKS & BIBLE STUDIES,
CALL TOLL FREE 1-800-366-7788 (USA)
or 1-416-499-4615 (CANADA)

C O N T E N T S

Introduction: Settling for Sour Grapes   7
The problem of reaching too far.

Crisispoint: The Myth of the Greener Grass   11
Facing the reasons for your dissatisfaction.

Evaluation: How Are You Feeling?   31
Test whether or not you're contented.

Bible Lessons:

1   Desperately Seeking More   37
   Counting the cost of greed.

2   Why Am I So Unhappy?   51
   The envious side of self-esteem.

3   Why Is Her Life So Good?   63
   When comparison leads to competition.

4   Please Don't Leave Me!   75
   The jealous feelings of loss.

Discussion: Is Her Life Really Better?   87
Questions for your small group.

Bibliography: Becoming the Real You   91
Books for study and growth.

In memory of
Frances Glover Storey,
who unwittingly passed
her writing gift
to granddaughters
and great-granddaughters.

ACKNOWLEDGMENTS

It's impossible to know why God allows one woman to live with better circumstances than another, or why she's born in one era instead of the next. Certainly, the advantages of each generation over the previous one can spark envy for women.

But I like to believe that if she'd lived long enough to meet us, my maternal grandmother would have discarded envy to applaud her descendants who write and publish. Given different circumstances in her life, I'm sure Frances Glover Storey would have been several books ahead of us anyway.

So we are grateful to carry Grandma's writing gift. And until we reach heaven to thank her for it, we'll continue her legacy on earth.

Special thanks to Helen McWhorter and others who prayed for me as I wrote this manuscript. ■

Settling for Sour Grapes

The problem of reaching too far.

Once upon a time, a fox who felt hungry and
thirsty stole into a vineyard and eyed some
sun-ripened grapes on a trellis.

"I'd give anything to have those grapes,"
he said with a watery mouth. But the grapes
hung beyond the fox's reach.

Still coveting the grapes, the fox ran
and jumped, snapping at the nearest bunch.
He missed. Again and again he jumped,
falling short of the grapes each time. Finally
exhausted and bitter, the fox crawled away
from the trellis.

"Well, I never really wanted those
grapes. They were probably sour and wormy
anyway," he complained.

The moral: Any fool can despise what he
cannot get.[1]

Aesop told this story generations ago,
but the moral still applies today. When we

7

covet something we can't obtain, life turns
into sour grapes. Especially when somebody
else has what we're striving for.

Many of us pass through times when
we ask, "Why is her life better than mine?"
Or, "Why does she get what I'm longing to
have? She's no better than me!" While we're
on earth, these questions elicit no definitive
answer. But they do point to what's rumbling
inside us.

We ask these questions because we're
envious or jealous. These two feelings,
though similar in their discontented nature,
leap from different motives. Yet their end
results are identical: They cause bitterness
and discontentment in us.

ABOUT THIS STUDY

If you've struggled against what you can't
have—especially when someone else has
it—then you'll benefit from this study
booklet. First, an article examines "The
Myth of Greener Grass" and the roots of
dissatisfaction. Then four Bible lessons
further explore envy and jealousy, and
how God wants to release you from their
debilitating grip.

You can use this study guide in many
ways. While it's best to read and study the
entire booklet, you may want to ponder just
the opening article. Or you might complete
only the Bible lessons. For these, you will
need a pen, a Bible, and sometimes a dictionary or concordance.

Whatever parts you study, consider using this guide for:

- Sunday school classes.

- Small-group Bible studies.

- Introducing women to Christ.

- One-on-one study or discipling.

- Personal study or devotional times.

- Professional or coffee-cup counseling.

However you use this study, remember that releasing yourself from dissatisfaction will be a process rather than an immediate turnaround. But with God's help, you can stop fretting about somebody else's life and begin reaching toward His design for you. ■

—JUDITH COUCHMAN

NOTE
1. *Aesop's Fables* (n.p.: Grosset & Dunlap, Publishers, 1947), page 18.

The Myth of
the Greener Grass

*Facing the reasons
for your dissatisfaction.*

"You sure do have a lot of cooking stuff," a
guest commented while glancing around my
kitchen.

"What do you mean?" I darted back. "I'm
in my thirties. Shouldn't I by now?"

"Well, a lot of people don't."

"That's probably because it doesn't matter to them. I've worked hard for this!"

We dropped the subject.

Interestingly, it wasn't the first time I'd
had that conversation. Close friends, dinner
guests, my mother, even packers from the
moving company had all commented on my
overstuffed kitchen. And for years I'd joked
about collecting enough kitchenware for
Julia Child.

So why this defensiveness? I asked
myself one night after the guests left.
Somewhere that evening, I'd sputtered

another "I don't have any more than any-one else" explanation. And I wondered why kitchen commentary bothered me so much.

A few weeks later, I found out.

Spotting the small envelope on my office desk, I complained inside, *Oh, no, another wedding-shower invitation.* Ripping it open, I confirmed my suspicion. It was my second shower invitation that month, and because of scheduling, I couldn't attend either one.

In moments, frustration descended. Not because I couldn't go. Or because neither woman was a close friend. Or because my finances were drooping. Or even because I think wedding showers border on the frivo-lous with those silly games. (I mean, how many times have you searched for small words in the "big" word wedding?)

It was something more, and after shop-ping for gifts, my attitude dawned on me. Wandering through the department store, no gift seemed "just right" for the soon-to-be-showered women. "Too predictable. Too expensive. Not her style," I muttered with each consideration.

Then I hit the kitchen department. And before long, I purchased a glass-domed cake holder and deliberated over a marked-down punch bowl set—for me. As far as the brides-to-be were concerned, I returned home empty-handed.

Rearranging for more space in the kitchen cupboard, I mentally justified my new purchase: *It was only ten dollars. I've been looking for one forever. I'm giving a dessert party next month.* But when I finally stuffed my cake holder on the shelf, I knew I was also jabbing all of the women whose wedding, baby, remarriage, and anniversary parties I'd attended for fifteen years.

I was tired of women who stocked their kitchens and linen closets by merely getting married. Of buying gift after gift, year after year, when I'd received none in return. Of pretending it didn't matter, when it really did.

So at least I admitted it. I was envious. Fortunate friends had made me defensive about my kitchen fortunes. And each "you have so much" comment came close to exposing my heart's attitude.

I wish I could say my envy sprang from a desire to be married. It didn't. It was the most selfish of all reasons: I wanted to receive free stuff, too. I also wish that now I joyfully rip open invitations and plot gift strategies. Actually, I attend few wedding showers. But I'm learning that big barriers to godliness often wrap themselves in small ingratitudes.

DESIRE TO POSSESS

"A man's life does not consist in the abundance of his possessions," said Jesus to the crowd gathered around Him (Luke 12:15). By implication, Jesus included women in His assessment. Or anything

13

else they might possess: beauty, talent, marriage, children, prestige, education, or relationships.

But it's difficult to remember that admonition when you're the woman without beauty or talent or a marriage or children or prestige or education or relationships or material possessions. And somebody you know has them.

Since humanity began, we've struggled to possess what we don't have. Nations fight for disputed land; children squabble over toys; coworkers resent the person who got promoted. From the petty to the earth shattering, it's difficult to stay content with what we have—and not to resent those with more than us. Unless arrested by God's Spirit, possessiveness grows into an insatiable desire.

"Mankind . . . esteem that which they have most desired as of no value the moment it is possessed, and torment themselves with fruitless wishes for which is beyond their reach," wrote Francois de la Mothe Fénélon, a seventeenth-century archbishop. He cited the cause as "the perverse depravity of their nature."[1]

With today's sophisticated mindset, it's uncomfortable to think of ourselves as "perverse" and "depraved." But if we truly believe God's Word, those descriptors fit our innermost hearts. Scripture says, "Everyone has turned away, they have together become corrupt; there is no one who does good, not even one" (Psalm 53:3).

In a short story called "Good Country People," Flannery O'Connor created a quirky traveling Bible salesman who visited a rural community. While selling Bibles he said, "The word of God ought to be in the parlor . . . for a Christian, the word of God ought to be in every room in the house besides in his heart."

But upon opening his valise in front of an atheistic girl, the salesman revealed a box of condoms, a flask of whiskey, an obscene deck of cards, and a lifestyle that mocked the Bibles he sold.

One day as two women knelt in a back pasture, digging up onions, they saw the salesman emerge from the woods and walk toward the highway.

"Why, that looks like the nice dull young man that tried to sell me a Bible yesterday," said Mrs. Hopewell. "He was so simple. I guess the world would be better off if we were all that simple."

"Some can't be that simple," replied her companion, Mrs. Freeman. "I know I never could."[2]

Without knowing about the salesman's mockery, Mrs. Freeman understood the basic nature of humans. On the outside we may exhibit virtue, but on the inside, we're stocked with the complicated attributes of sin. We can cry with the apostle Paul, "What a wretched man I am! Who will rescue me from this body of [sin and] death?" (Romans 7:24).

So when we lust after a friend's silver coffee set, bedroom furniture suite, or wonderfully attentive husband, it's not these external advantages that lure us. Rather, we're tempted from within by our sinful souls. "Each one is tempted when, by his own evil desire, he is dragged away and enticed," wrote James to early Christians. "Then, after desire has conceived, it gives birth to sin" (James 1:14-15).

When we want something that belongs to someone else, we're coveting. God felt so strongly about this sin that it's included in the Ten Commandments: "You shall not covet your neighbor's house. You shall not covet your neighbor's wife, or his manservant or maidservant, his ox or donkey, or anything that belongs to your neighbor" (Exodus 20:17). Roughly translated, coveting anything that belongs to anyone else is sin.

In my mind, the neighborhood garage sale models our basic desire to possess what belongs to someone else. Somehow, when it's arranged on tables in the stark sunlight, other people's junk looks more enticing than our own. Hosting my first driveway sale with a friend, I remember how this startled me.

That morning, I encountered the "early birds"—people who arrived an hour before the sale began and peered, vulture-like, at our castoffs. Slightly irritated, I sloughed off my surprise to a lack of experience. But the real vexation descended when people haggled over my already rock-bottom prices. Examining a man's shirt marked at fifty cents, a guy said, "This is too much. How about twenty-five cents for it?"

Everything inside of me wanted to ask, "Do you know what *quality* you're getting? Do you know how much this *originally* cost?" But I swallowed my pride. My friend Lou and I joked that people not only lusted after our things, but they wanted them on their own stingy terms.

Still, we were the biggest laugh when the sale ended. Counting up the day's receipts, Lou discovered she owed more money than she'd earned. She'd bought so many of my things, her sales totaled a negative balance. And to this day, I look at her objects in my home and ask, "Whatever prompted me to buy this?"

Scripturally, I know the answer. But I still struggle when, for example, my mother is giving away some things to me and my sisters and I try to be fair to them.

EARTHLY STEWARDSHIP

In reality, the idea of a Christian "owning" anything is a misnomer. David declared, "The earth is the LORD's, and everything in it, the world, and all who live in it" (Psalm 24:1). When we covet someone else's possessions, we're lusting after what really belongs to God.

Jesus taught about the dangers of putting too much stock into what doesn't belong to us anyway:

"The ground of a certain rich young man produced a good crop. He thought to himself, 'What shall I do? I have no place to put my crops.'

"Then he said, 'This is what I'll do. I will tear down my barns and build bigger ones, and there I will store all my grain and my goods. And I'll say to myself, "You have plenty of good things laid up for many years. . . .'"

"But God said to him, 'You fool! This very night your life will be demanded from you. Then who will get what you have prepared for yourself?'

"This is how it will be with anyone who stores up things for himself but is not rich toward God." (Luke 12:16-21)

When we continually focus on possessions, we can gradually rape ourselves of communion with God. It's frightening to think that a negative definition of *possession* applies to evil spirits as well as to us. In this sense, only the Holy Spirit can possess without hurting the possessor or the possession. How sad that the more we try to clutch anything, the more we risk crumbling our inner selves. How tragic that we want to possess other people's things, too.

ENJOYING GIFTS

On the flip side, we can become so ascetic that we fail to enjoy the things God entrusts to us. In the movie *Babette's Feast*, set in

the late 1800s, filmmakers fleshed out Isak
Dinesen's story about a pious congregation
on the desolate coast of Denmark. In this
story, two elderly, unmarried sisters took in a
French woman who fled her country's unrest.
Babette became the sisters' cook and house-
keeper, preparing the codfish and ale-bread
soup they requested each day.

For fourteen years, the three women
existed together, denying themselves not
much more than church meetings and knit-
ting. But life momentarily changed when
Babette won the French lottery. She decided
to spend her winnings on a sumptuous feast
for the townsfolk, who thought she'd gone
mad and denounced her cooking as sin.
Before the dinner, they covenanted to say
nothing about the food.

Babette prepared the several-course
feast—a celebration of artistic cooking—and
the townspeople, though they obviously
enjoyed the food, never commented on it.
They also failed to realize this dinner's
effects on them: It melted the bitterness that
entrapped their relationships.

When the guests left, Babette revealed
to her employers that she once was the master chef at the finest restaurant in Paris. Yet
other than the two sisters, the people held
no regard for the great gift Babette bestowed
on them.

In the same way, we can miss enjoying the gifts that God gives to us. James
said, "Every good and perfect gift is from
above, coming down from the Father" (James

1:17). He bestows these gifts because of His great love for us.

So rather than obsessing about and clinging to possessions, God wants us to be glad and wise stewards of what we're given (Luke 12:42-44). Typically, stewards manage properties generously entrusted to them, but do not claim ownership. In our materialistic society, this is a tricky balance to keep.

ENVY VERSUS JEALOUSY

Our desire to possess can focus on people as well as objects. And herein lies the distinction between envy and jealousy. We are envious of things we don't have; we are jealous of people who might rob what we already own. Dictionaries distinguish between envy and jealousy this way:

> **Envy:** *Feelings of discontent and ill will because of another's advantages, possessions, etc.; resentful dislike of another who has something that one desires.*[3]

> **Jealousy:** *The state of mind arising from the suspicion, apprehension, or knowledge of rivalry.*[4]

Jealousy is also the fear of being supplanted in the affection, or distrust of the fidelity, of a beloved person.

Whether we're wanting to possess things or people, the desire can stir the sinful nature within us. We feel resentful, bitter, vindictive. And we often harm ourselves deeper than the people we covet or distrust.

"For years, I coveted the accomplishments of a woman in my industry," a colleague told me. "She had it all: a superb job, a polished appearance, award-winning work, a devoted husband, darling kids, and more money than I'll ever make. And everybody loved her. In contrast, everything I wanted seemed to dissipate.

"But then one day it struck me: I was torn up inside from envy and competition with this woman—and she had no idea! She was continuing her life, miles away in another state, and I was eating up myself over her. That's when I realized I was the one with the problem, not her. And I asked God to forgive and to change me."

RUINED RELATIONSHIPS

My colleague wrestled with envy: wanting what someone else has. Conversely, jealousy protrudes when we're protecting what we already have. When we too tenaciously guard our possessions and relationships, we often hurt ourselves instead of the rivals we fear. The storyteller Aesop exemplified this fatal point in "Jupiter and the Bee."

According to this tale, an industrious bee stored her honeycombs from a bountiful harvest. Then she flew to the god Jupiter to offer him a gift of fresh nectar. Delighted with her offering, Jupiter promised the bee whatever she desired.

"Please give me a stinger, so I can kill anyone who approaches my hive to take the honey," begged the bee.

This bloodthirsty request surprised and enraged Jupiter. "Your request is granted," he said. "When anyone tries to take away your honey, the wound shall be fatal. Except it shall be fatal to you. Your life will cease with the sting."[5]

Likewise, when we're stridently jealous, we can psychologically and spiritually wound ourselves with broken relationships. Many of us know the painful loss of a beloved person to whom we clung to so much, we drove the individual away.

My first big love ended like that. At seventeen, I hadn't learned that relationships must be held with an open hand—that squeezing too hard ensures their death. Instead, I jealously obsessed and possessed until finally he left me. It took years to understand that dependence masquerades as love.

By digging deep, we discover that envy and jealousy root themselves in doubts about ourselves and God. To understand, we must more closely examine each of these feelings.

ENVY'S GREED

If we truly believe in God's all-knowing map for our lives, then envy slaps at His sovereignty. When we're envious, we tell the Creator that He doesn't know what's best for us, that we'd rather have what's "on the other side of the fence."

This concept struck home for me when, after complaining about what I hadn't obtained in life yet, my mother replied, "I believe you have everything that God has intended for you so far." It was a sobering thought—a comment that made me reassess my expectations.

When we honestly think about it, nobody's life "on the other side of the fence" is as wonderful as it looks. If we jumped to the "greener grass," we'd find problems there, too. A friend recently told me, "If you want the greener grass, you have to put up with a lot of manure." Many of our notions about someone's "better life" disregard unpleasant realities.

Part of the reason we'd find difficulties on "the other side" rests in selfishness—our own greed that breeds unhappiness wherever we go. With greed in control, we live by the principle, "If only I had one more thing, then I'd be happy." In her book *Living on Less and Liking It More*, Maxine Hancock described this process:

> *All of these sighs of "if only" fail to take into account that as we move into that bigger house, as we earn that larger income, as we wear the new coat, as we walk on that new rug, we are still basically the same people. And the inward sigh of bitterness and discontent . . .*

23

*will still be on our lips, but with another
ending. . . .*

*Any concept of contentment which
is linked to specific things is a fallacy.
The person who thinks that some specific
thing finally will bring him to that pla-
teau called contentment is being deluded
by Satan, that master deceiver who since
the Garden of Eden has been whispering
his urgings to the human heart to reach,
reach, reach, and take.*[6]

Instead of always reaching, God wants
to teach us contentment. The apostle Paul
told the Philippians, "I have learned to be
content whatever the circumstances. . . . I
have learned the secret of being content in
any and every situation, whether well fed or
hungry, whether living in plenty or in want. I
can do everything through him who gives me
strength" (Philippians 4:11-13).

Even for this great Christian, contentment was a learned response, dependent on
supernatural help. Yet contentment didn't
mean continually living with deprivation. It
meant fully appreciating what he had, when
he had it, and taking his eyes off the hori-
zon—or off other people's goods.

BECOMING OURSELVES

To be content, we also need to take our eyes
off self-degradation. When we envy others,
we're not content with who we are, or more
accurately, who God made us to be. Envying

another person's attributes also leads to trouble. Eventually, we can unconsciously try to be that other person—or at least try to be who we are not.

In his award-winning children's book, *Fables,* author and illustrator Arnold Lobel told the story of a Wolf who posed as an apple tree:

> *One October day, a Hen looked out her window. She saw an apple tree growing in her backyard.*
>
> *"Now that is odd," said the Hen. "I am certain that there was no tree standing in that spot yesterday."*
>
> *"There are some of us that grow fast," said the tree.*
>
> *"I have never seen a tree," she said, "that has ten furry toes."*
>
> *"There are some of us that do," said the tree. "Hen, come outside and enjoy the cool shade of my leafy branches."*

The Hen continued questioning the tree about its long, pointed ears and mouth of sharp teeth, but the Wolf still didn't reveal himself. Then she hit on another idea:

> *"I have heard," said the Hen, "that some of you trees lose all of your leaves at this time of the year."*
>
> *"Oh, yes," said the tree, "there are some of us that will." The tree began to quiver and shake. All of its leaves quickly dropped off.*

The Hen was not surprised to see a large Wolf in the place where an apple tree had been standing just a moment before. She locked her shutters and slammed her window closed.

The Wolf . . . stormed away in an angry rage.[7]

Lobel's moral to the story: "It is always difficult to pose as something that one is not."[8] When we try to be like someone else, we can look as ridiculous as Lobel's hairy Wolf. We gather the dismay of those around us and, in the end, wind up angry because our disguise doesn't work. How much better to be fully who we are rather than trying to fit someone else's skin. Understanding this plays a vital role in the demise of greed and the arrival of contentment.

JEALOUSY'S DEPENDENCE

While envy strives to acquire what somebody else has, out-of-control jealousy tries to possess the other person or thing altogether. When we're overtly jealous, it may be we're unable to individuate ourselves. That is, we're incapable of accepting our value as a separate individual. Our identity is wrapped up in, and totally dependent on, somebody or something else.

I use the words "out-of-control" and "overtly" to describe this feeling because there is a healthy jealousy that protects against harm. God is jealous of anything that

26

diverts our worship of Him (Deuteronomy 5:9-10). A mother jealously guards her child's safety. A marriage needs its partners to watch jealously for ways to strengthen their bond. These are necessary, normal ways of nurturing relationships.

Yet under the guise of nurturance, jealousy can spin into a binding, suffocating noose. We can become overly watchful and obviously resentful of the beloved's time away from us, or the threat of losing possessions. We can even subvert those who, if only in our minds, might take the beloved person or thing away from us.

Ironically, uncontrolled jealousy eventually turns on the beloved. We grow bitter toward the person who doesn't meet our every need, our every expectation for an intimate or exclusive relationship. We begin to despise the job that we compete to gain and scramble to protect. We become irritated with our children who would rather play with friends than spend time with us. News reports and classic plays tell us that crimes of passion are jealousy run amok.

In her self-revealing book *Jealousy*, author Nancy Friday surmised that "people who have separation problems are the ones who suffer that sapping, sinking sense of isolation, humiliation, defeat. We are the ones who suspect betrayal where none exists. We are the jealous ones."[9]

Although Friday expanded her definition of those who feel jealous, there's still fundamental truth in her supposition. When we fail to separate ourselves as individuals—as lovable and valuable in our own right—jealousy can consume us. As with envy, we lack confidence in who we are, in who God made us to be. We need somebody or something else to bolster our faith in His unique creation.

If we allow it, we can use jealousy to throw us back to dependence on God. The threat of real or imagined loss can cause us to rediscover Him as our only source of security, as the only One who can't be consumed by our jealous pursuit. Putting God in His rightful place—at the center of our hearts—is the key to conquering jealousy.

FINAL ANALYSIS

In the final analysis, envy and jealousy aren't the fault of a misguided God or people who possess more than us. These feelings originate from a sinful, distorted view of ourselves and our belongings. And with God's help, that perspective can change.

We can freely love God and who He made us to be; we can feel content with what we have; we can practice stewardship as a means of taking care of the earth and the things in it; we can halt our unhealthy competition; we can build relationships without jealous dependence. So whatever side of the fence we're on, we can stop lusting after the "greener grass" and live as though "godliness with contentment is great gain" (1 Timothy 6:6). ■

NOTES

1. Frank S. Mead, *The Encyclopedia of Religious Quotations* (Old Tappan, NJ: Fleming H. Revell Company, 1965), page 331.
2. Flannery O'Connor, *A Good Man Is Hard to Find and Other Stories* (New York: Harcourt Brace Jovanovich, Publishers, 1976), pages 193-196.
3. David B. Guralink, ed., *Webster's New World Dictionary* (New York: Simon and Schuster, 1982), page 468.
4. C. T. Onions, ed., *The Shorter Oxford English Dictionary*, vol. 1 (Oxford, Great Britain: Oxford University Press, 1973), page 1129.
5. *Aesop's Fables* (n.p.: Grosset & Dunlap, Inc., 1947), page 74.
6. Maxine Hancock, *Living on Less and Liking It More* (Chicago, IL: Moody Press, 1976), pages 33-34.
7. Arnold Lobel, *Fables* (New York: Harper & Row, Publishers, 1980), page 11.
8. *Fables*, page 11.
9. Nancy Friday, *Jealousy* (New York: Bantam Books, 1987), page 15.

How Are You Feeling?

*Test whether or not
you're contented.*

Are you content with yourself, your life, your possessions, your relationships? This test can help you decide.

CONTENTMENT TEST

1. For each statement, circle the number below the word that most accurately reflects your feelings, when 1=never; 2=seldom; 3=sometimes; 4=often; 5=always. (All references to jealousy refer to unhealthy responses.)

   a. I am happy with the abilities God gave to me.   1 2 3 4 5

   b. I do not compare my appearance or clothes to other women.

                                     1 2 3 4 5

31

c. I am satisfied with my home and its
furnishings. 1 2 3 4 5

d. I am free from jealousy toward sib-
lings or other members of my family.
1 2 3 4 5

e. I feel joy for friends, family, and
others who get what they want,
even though I may not obtain what
I desire. 1 2 3 4 5

f. I am satisfied with my marital status.
1 2 3 4 5

g. I am free from jealousy about my husband or boyfriend.
1 2 3 4 5

h. I accept the members of my family as
they are and feel no urge to change
them. 1 2 3 4 5

i. I compliment people without feeling
envious. 1 2 3 4 5

j. I appreciate what other women have
accomplished, without comparing
myself to them. 1 2 3 4 5

k. I do my best, without competing with
other people.
1 2 3 4 5

l. I am satisfied that other people have better jobs than me.

1 2 3 4 5

m. I am free from worry about losing important relationships with friends.

1 2 3 4 5

n. I am grateful for the circumstances of my life.   1 2 3 4 5

o. My household income is enough.

1 2 3 4 5

p. I share what I have with others (food, money, possessions).

1 2 3 4 5

q. I shop with moderation.

1 2 3 4 5

r. I do not feel jealous about my children's relationships with other people.

1 2 3 4 5

s. I purchase what I need and can afford, not necessarily what is "the best" or better than anyone else.

1 2 3 4 5

t. I do not worry about getting everything I want.   1 2 3 4 5

u. I feel good about what I have obtained in life so far.

1 2 3 4 5

v. I thank God for what He's given to me.
1 2 3 4 5

2. a. Total the number of circles you made
in each column.

1   2   3   4   5

Totals: ___ ___ ___ ___ ___

b. Multiply each response number by the
number of times you circled it.

RESPONSE		NUMBER OF CIRCLES	SUBTOTALS
1	x	_____	_____
2	x	_____	_____
3	x	_____	_____
4	x	_____	_____
5	x	_____	_____

c. Add these subtotals together for a
grand total.

Grand Total: _____

3. Based on the grand total, circle the category you fit into below.

TOTAL   CONTENTMENT RATING

22-43   You are unhappy with your life
and envious or jealous of
others.

44-65   You need to prayerfully
        guard against envious or jealous
        attitudes.

66-87   You try to keep people, posses-
        sions, and circumstances in
        perspective.

88-110 You are a contented person.

YOUR RESPONSES

4. Do you agree or disagree with your
   contentment rating? Explain.

5. Review the statements, a to v, and your
   responses to them. Put a check by the
   responses you want to change.

6. a. From the article, "The Myth of the
      Greener Grass," on pages 11-29, copy
      statements that would be helpful as
      you work toward changing.

b. Incorporate the above statements into a prayer, asking God to help you change. Write it below.

7. In addition to completing the following lessons, list three things you could do immediately to begin changing your actions and attitudes.

UPCOMING LESSONS

Now you're ready to start the Bible studies. Each lesson begins with an excerpt or real-life story to help you identify your own struggle with envy or jealousy. Then Bible passages help you understand God's viewpoint on these feelings.

Are you ready to find out more? If so, turn the page and begin. ■

Desperately Seeking More

Counting the cost of greed.

Author and teacher Maxine Hancock says she and her husband, Cam, grew up in the "good old days when credit was the magic key that unlocked all the goodies that adults could have."[1]

Read how the days turned "not so good" when the Hancocks dove into debt:

THE MERRY-GO-ROUND

I was expecting our first child and had time to turn the pages of the fat catalogs which, for people in rural areas like ours, served as department stores. And, with my shiny new credit cards, I was able to charge the things we needed. I'm sure that everything I bought was quite legitimate and defensible. I know I never shopped frivolously.

But I remember the sudden shock and

*panic that struck me when, after the delight
of numbers of little parcels arriving in the
mail, the statements followed. I could hardly
imagine that the "few little things" I bought
had pushed the balance on our two accounts
to a combined $300.*

*The other shock came over the next few
months. Do you know how long it takes to
reduce a balance of $300 at the minimum
monthly payment of $12? Forever. At least,
it seems that long. Especially if you happen
to add a thing or two to that account as you
go along.*

*I was learning that the exciting consumer
concept of revolving credit was a merry-go-
round with the music stuck in an endless,
mindless ditty of "buy now, and pay and pay
and pay." It was a merry-go-round that never
had to stop at all.*

MONTHLY STATEMENTS

*Worst of all, the monthly statements had
a way of coming out to coincide with the
time when most average people were bring-
ing home their paychecks. But we had no
paycheck. Just those big, tantalizing lump
sums that came with shipping a load of pigs
or selling a bin of grain—those big checks
that all seemed to be paid out to the men who
had delivered our gas, stockpiled our ferti-
lizer, or sold us seed.*

*It was hard to scratch up enough, on a
month-to-month basis, to pay even the mini-
mum payments on those charge accounts.*

*And if there's one thing I cannot face, it's a
dunner. "We hope that your failure to make
a payment last month was an oversight.
However, terms of our credit agreement with
you stipulate that if we do not receive your
payment of _____ by _____ , we shall
_____."*

*Those notes devastated me. Not that we
were defaulting in any long-term way. As
soon as there was money, we paid the back
payment and one or two in advance. We sim-
ply limped from lump to lump. And between
times, I would find myself having to charge
something or other, pushing up that balance
once again. It finally dawned on me that the
whole principle of the revolving credit system
was that you should never get a balance paid
off. You should always have a balance, pay
interest on it, pay off some and add on some.*

*And about the same time, it dawned on
me that it was those monthly accounts that
made me most unhappy and most discontent.*
                                    —Maxine Hancock[2]

NEED VERSUS GREED

1. Although Maxine was not a frivolous
   shopper, what desires did credit fulfill
   for her?

2. a. Besides credit, how does our society tempt us toward owning more and more possessions?

   b. By which of these are you most tempted?

3. a. Using a dictionary, define the following terms.

   To need:

   To be greedy:

   b. From these definitions, describe the difference between *a need* and *greed*.

4. Do you think most people recognize their greed? Why, or why not?

GREEDY STORIES

5. a. For each of the following Bible characters, indicate what the person(s) desired and the result of greediness.

DESIRE	RESULT
Adam and Eve (Genesis 3)	
Samuel's Sons (1 Samuel 8:1-6)	

DESIRE	RESULT
False Prophets (Isaiah 56:10-12)	
Ananias and Sapphira (Acts 5:1-10)	

b. Do you think greed always reaps bad
   results? Explain.

6. What warnings do the following verses
   give about greediness? What is suggested
   to replace greed?

WARNING	REPLACEMENT
Luke 12:15,22-23	
Ephesians 5:3,8-10	
Hebrews 13:5	

7. a. In what ways might we camouflage our greediness?

b. According to Jeremiah 17:10 and Luke 12:2-3, what happens to "hidden" sins?

8. Reread the parable in Luke 12:16-21, on page 18 in this booklet. Then answer these questions by checking "yes" or "no" to indicate your insights to this passage. Explain your reason for each response.

YES NO
❏ ❏ It was wrong for this man to be rich.

❏ ❏ The rich man was justified in building bigger barns.

❏ ❏ The rich man had the right motivation for obtaining more.

❏ ❏ Wealthy people can be rich toward God.

❏ ❏ God always rewards greediness with death.

9. According to Ephesians 4:17-19, what happens when greediness continues unchecked?

10. What do you think are the motivations behind greed?

11. According to the following verses, how does greed originate in our lives?

Numbers 14:18

James 1:14-15

1 John 2:15-16

12. Read the parables Jesus told about stewards in Luke 12:42-48 and 16:1-8. Then answer the following questions, drawing conclusions based on these stories.

   a. What is a steward's job?

   b. What makes a steward valuable?

   c. What benefits does a steward receive?

   d. How can a steward act foolishly?

13. Do you think we should consider ourselves stewards and not owners of possessions? List three reasons for your response.

14. a. Read Luke 16:10-12. What is the result of good stewardship? Of poor stewardship?

    b. What was Christ's warning about money in verse 13? (Some translations say "unrighteous mammon.")

15. Look at another of Jesus' stories, the parable of the talents, in Matthew 25:14-29 and consider its implications. As you read, view the money (talents) as a symbol for personal abilities and talents. Then answer the following questions:

47

a. How are talents and abilities part of what we possess?

b. What are appropriate uses of our talents and abilities?

c. What are inappropriate uses of our talents and abilities?

d. How can we become greedy with our talents and abilities?

e. How can we avoid such greed?

f. What is the result of good stewardship of our talents and abilities?

16. From the verses and parables you have read, write a "policy statement" from God about how believers should view and use their possessions (things, talents, abilities, etc.).

YOUR STEWARDSHIP

17. How does your attitude toward possessions compare to the "policy statement" you wrote for question 16? Indicate how you do and do not align with it.

18. How can you ensure your own biblical stewardship? List several actions you can take.

SERIOUS BUSINESS

This week, consider again how greed originates in our hearts. (See question 10.) Using your Bible and a concordance, prayerfully investigate how to turn from the sin of greed. It would be helpful to explore *confession, repentance, spiritual warfare,* and *forgiveness.*[3]

After completing this word study, make a step-by-step game plan for tackling your greed. ∎

NOTES
1. Maxine Hancock, *Living on Less and Liking It More* (Chicago, IL: Moody Press, 1976), page 58. Used by permission.
2. Hancock, pages 59-61.
3. Another CRISISPOINTS study, *Getting a Grip on Guilt,* explores these topics (NavPress, 1990).

Why Am I
So Unhappy?

The envious side of self-esteem.

As a youth, my friend Jim learned about an
unexpected effect of envy: It can hurt the
envious person more than the envied person.
Read Jim's story:

JIM'S STORY

*During my youth, I had a close friend, Pete,
who had a charismatic personality. And, in
my mind, his was much more appealing and
humorous than mine. I felt mine was rather
dull by comparison.*

*Eventually my envy began to crop up
toward Pete, causing my mind to fixate on
his personality. Particularly when we were
together, I dwelled on the obvious contrast
between his personality and mine, much to
the exclusion of positive, wholesome thoughts.*

Consequently, anger swelled within,

51

forcing me to fixate even more, leading to increased envy, and thereby closing the vicious circle.

Next, with this vicious circle remaining unchecked, my periodic bouts of anger turned into a solid root of bitterness toward Pete. Driven by a resulting instinct to get even with him, I began to emotionally cut myself off from him, which, one day, led to the sudden, unexplained termination of the relationship.

Prior to this termination, though, I became embittered toward myself as well as Pete for falling, as far as personality was concerned, into his shadow. Then, agitated by my seeming deficiency, I became increasingly self-critical as a form of self-directed attack. Thus, when speaking of the havoc envy produces in the mind and relationships, I can speak painfully from personal experience.

—James Hilt[2]

LOOKING AT JIM'S STORY

1. a. Once Jim gave in to envy, what other negative emotions surfaced?

   b. How might Jim have avoided these attitudes and actions?

52

c. What was the root cause of Jim's envy?

2. a. Think of a time when you envied someone else. In the boxes below, write the personal attitudes and actions that followed envy and created your vicious cycle.

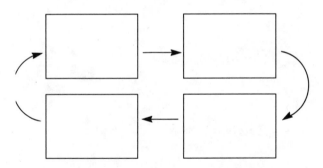

b. What were the results of this cycle?

c. What was the root cause of your envy?

   d. How do you think this root cause developed?

GOD'S VIEWPOINT

3. In the Bible verses that follow, what other sinful actions and feelings are associated with envy?

   Romans 1:28-32

   1 Timothy 6:3-5

   Titus 3:3

4. Why would envy be listed with what we might consider as "drastic" or "serious" sins?

5. According to James 2:10, does God differentiate among sins the way we do? Explain.

6. a. In the Old Testament, God warned against coveting other people's things. In your own words, write out the command presented in Deuteronomy 5:21.

   b. Why do you think God mentioned that these specific people and things should not be coveted?

   c. Do you think coveting applies only to the things mentioned in this command? Explain.

7. Why do you think God spoke so strongly against covetousness? See Colossians 3:5-10.

8. a. According to Romans 7:7-13, why did God give us the law, "Do not covet"?

   b. What were the results of the law's instruction?

   c. What does this result reveal about humanity's basic nature?

9. According to Romans 13:8-10, how does God want to replace our covetousness?

10. What barriers could exist in ridding ourselves of covetousness?

11. In addition to the actions of question 9, in what other ways can we rid ourselves of covetousness?

Philippians 4:8

1 John 1:9

1 John 2:15-17

12. According to the following verses, what could happen if covetousness continues?

Matthew 24:12

1 Timothy 6:10

INSIDE YOU

13. Reflect back on the article, "The Myth of the Greener Grass," on pages 11-29. What personal problems/attitudes could cause you to envy/covet?

14. How is your opinion of yourself connected to envy/coveting?

15. a. In the chart, list the ways you're discontented with yourself. Then list the things that you envy/covet in others.

DISCONTENTMENT/SELF	ENVY/ OTHERS

b. Do you see correlations between these lists? If so, what are they?

LOVING YOURSELF

16. a. According to the following verses, how does God want you to view yourself?

Psalm 17:8

Psalm 139:14

Ephesians 5:1-2

   b. If you lived according to these verses, how could it affect the envy/covetousness that you feel?

17. a. How can you begin believing and living out God's viewpoint of you? In the chart, list three things you want to believe and what you can do to "own" them for yourself.

TO BELIEVE	TO DO

b. How can you begin to erase the envy/covetousness from your life? List three things you can do.

LEARNING TO LOVE

This week, use a Bible concordance to locate verses about how we should love one another. Then answer the following questions:

- Why is love important in the Body of Christ?

- How is a lack of love related to envy and coveting?

- How do we express love to one another?

- How can you learn to love other people? Yourself? ■

NOTE
1. James Hilt, *How to Have a Better Relationship With Anybody* (Chicago, IL: Moody Press, 1984), pages 72-73. Used by permission.

Why Is Her Life So Good?

*When comparison leads
to competition.*

As a professor and leader of small groups,
Em Griffin has observed many relational
styles. One of the most damaging has been
competition. Read what he has written about
this mindset:

POWER PLAYS

*The Allies won a clear victory in World War 1.
But the harsh Treaty of Versailles sowed the
seeds of World War 2.*

*. . . [As a teacher,] that could happen
to me. "Look, you crummy students, I'm the
teacher here. If you don't like the way I run
my class, get out. I spent four years of gradu-
ate work getting a Ph.D., and I've taught this
course for ten years. No lousy sophomore is
going to tell me how to write a test."*

Of course I'd never use those words or

*present it in that mood and manner, but
sometimes I've echoed those sentiments. A
teacher's got big guns and ammunition. It's
tempting to use the power position to mow
down the opposition. But of course it doesn't
stifle dissent, it merely drives it underground
where it can fester.*

*I think there's a certain personality that
revels in competition. (I know I used to be
this way.) I'm not talking about enjoying a
friendly game of tennis, but rather the com-
pulsive desire to win an argument for the
sake of winning. Jaw stuck out, eyes burn-
ing, all the issues are black and white, good
or bad. . . . [We think] differences between
people need to be erased through persuasion
or force, and we know just the one to clean
the slate.*

*All in all, it doesn't appear to be a
healthy approach [to relationships].*

—Em Griffin[1]

COMPETITIVE CULTURE

1. Think about Em's imagined power struggle with his students. Why would he
   engage in this kind of competition?

2. a. What motivations cause people to compete with each other?

   b. How does our culture encourage competition? How do you feel about this?

   c. What feelings and actions, negative and positive, result from competition?

COMPARING OURSELVES

3. a. Generally, competition is based on comparing ourselves with others. Read the following biblical accounts of people who competed with each other. Describe the comparison that was made, the competition that ensued, and the obvious or implied results.

COMPARISON & COMPETITION	OBVIOUS OR IMPLIED RESULTS
Esau and Jacob (Genesis 27:1-41)	
Rachel and Leah (Genesis 30:1-24)	

COMPARISON & COMPETITION	OBVIOUS OR IMPLIED RESULTS
Mary and Martha (Luke 10:38-42)	

b. In these Bible passages, did both people have to compare and compete to cause problems? Explain.

c. How can comparison and competition lead to sin?

d. Why do you think these narratives were included in the Bible?

4. Choose one of the narratives and—as with envy in lesson 2, question 2—create a vicious cycle that resulted from comparison and competition. Write the attitudes and actions in the boxes below. (You might also include what you've learned about greed, envy, and covetousness.)

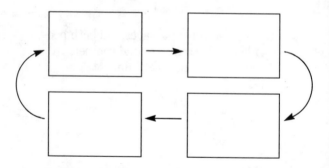

5. What causes people to compare themselves with others?

6. What does 2 Corinthians 10:12 say about "comparing ourselves with ourselves"?

7. a. Are there incidences where comparing ourselves with others is healthy and beneficial? Explain and give examples.

   b. What do you see as the differentiating characteristics between healthy and unhealthy comparisons?

PERSONAL COMPARISONS

8. a. Over what things are you most inclined to compare yourself with others?

b. Why do you think this is so?

9. Think of someone you compare yourself
   with, past or present, and answer these
   questions.

   a. Why do you compare yourself with
      this person?

   b. What feelings does comparison with
      this person stir in you?

   c. Have you benefited from these com-
      parisons? Why, or why not?

d. How do these comparisons affect the other person?

10. Create your own cycle of feelings and actions when you compare yourself to this person.

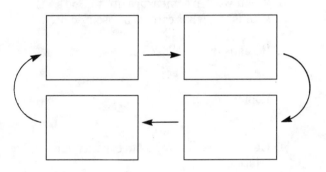

TRUE MEASUREMENTS

11. What or whom should be the believer's "measuring stick" of comparison?

Psalm 119:105

1 Corinthians 2:12-16

12. According to Romans 3:23 and Ephesians 2:8-9, to what degree can we measure up to God's standard on our own merit? Why?

13. When we don't "measure up" to God's standards, what can we be assured of?

    Romans 3:21-22,24-25

    Romans 4:4-8

14. How does God want us to conduct our relationships?

    Ephesians 4:32–5:2

    Colossians 3:12-17

15. What can happen when we make comparisons part of relationships? (See 2 Corinthians 12:20.)

16. How do our expectations for ourselves
    and for others relate to competition?

17. Based on what you've learned in this
    lesson, list actions, attitudes, and feelings
    you can use as a "measuring stick" when
    you make unhealthy comparisons that
    lead to destructive competition.

    a. I am making unhealthy compari-
       sons when:

       I feel like . . .

       I do these things . . .

       I think that . . .

b. I am competing in a destructive
   way when:

   I feel like . . .

   I do these things . . .

   I think that . . .

CHARTING COMPETITION

This week, use these measuring sticks to
determine whether you're making unhealthy
comparisons and destructively competing
with others. At the end of the week, answer
these questions:

   • Can you identify a pattern of feelings
     and actions?

   • What caused you to compare and/or to
     compete?

   • How did you feel after each incident?

   • How did it affect relationships? ∎

NOTE
1. Em Griffin, *Getting Together: A Guide for Good
   Groups* (Downers Grove, IL: InterVarsity Press, 1982),
   pages 146-147.

Please Don't Leave Me!

The jealous feelings of loss.

In his book *Love Must Be Tough*, psychologist Dr. James Dobson described a typical North American couple who entered marriage with different expectations. Read and consider this excerpt from his bestselling book:

RESENTING TIME AWAY

Young John is out there competing like crazy in the marketplace, thinking his successes are automatically appreciated by the lady at home. To his shock, she not only fails to notice, but even seems to resent the work that takes him from her.

"I'm doing it for you, babe!" he says. Diane isn't convinced.

What gradually develops from that misunderstanding is a deep, abiding anger

*on Diane's part, and a bewildered disgust
from John.*

*The wife is convinced that her low self-
esteem and her unhappiness are the result of
her husband's romantic failures. With every
year that passes, she becomes more bitter and
hostile at him for giving so little of himself to
his family. She attacks him viciously for what
she considers to be his deliberate insults, and
bludgeons him for refusing to change.*

*John, on the other hand, does not have
it within him to satisfy her needs. He didn't
see it modeled by his father and his mascu-
line, competitive temperament is not given to
romantic endeavors. Besides, his work takes
every ounce of energy in his body. It is a total
impasse. There seems to be no way around it.*

—James Dobson[1]

SORTING OUT

1. a. Do you think John and Diane are jus-
      tified in their responses to each other?
      Why, or why not?

   b. What are the motivations behind John
      and Diane's responses?

c. If they don't break the impasse,
   what else could happen to their
   relationship?

JEALOUS LOSS

2. Jealous feelings are often connected to a
   feared or actual loss of a beloved person.
   In the following biblical accounts, what
   kinds of losses were these people facing?
   Of whom could these people have felt
   jealous?

TYPE OF LOSS	JEALOUS RESPONSE
Hannah (1 Samuel 1:1-11)	
Job's Wife (Job 1:13-19, 2:7-9)	

TYPE OF LOSS	JEALOUS RESPONSE
Christ's Mother (Luke 8:19-21)	

3. a. In addition to jealousy, what other feelings could have resulted from these people's losses?

   b. Do you think losses like these would yield healthy or unhealthy jealousy, or both? Explain.

HEALTHY JEALOUSY

4. a. In these biblical statements, what kind of healthy jealousy was expressed?

   Exodus 34:14

2 Corinthians 11:2-3

b. In your opinion, are there other
   types of healthy jealousy? If so, what
   are they?

5. How might you distinguish between
   healthy and unhealthy jealousy?

UNHEALTHY JEALOUSY

6. In these biblical stories, what kind of
   unhealthy jealousy was expressed?

   David and Saul
   (1 Samuel 18:5-15)

Two Mothers
(1 Kings 3:16-27)

7. What do you think characterizes
   unhealthy jealousy?

8. When we feel unhealthy jealousy, what
   is wrong with our focus in life? (See
   Deuteronomy 6:4-7 and Matthew 6:33.)

9. How might unhealthy jealousy affect
   self-esteem?

10. What can be the response of the person
    of whom we feel jealous?

11. a. What seems to be jealousy's main objective?

    b. Do you think this objective is usually reached? Why, or why not?

12. a. From what you've learned in this booklet, how is jealousy related to greed, envy, comparison, and competition?

    b. Does fear play a role in jealousy? Explain.

CONQUERING JEALOUSY

13. According to these references, how can we overcome jealousy?

Acts 8:22-23

Romans 12:9-21

Hebrews 12:14-15

14. a. In the chart, list the people of whom
you feel jealous. What is each person's
response? What response are you
seeking?

PERSON & RESPONSE	DESIRED RESPONSE

PERSON & RESPONSE	DESIRED RESPONSE

b. In these relationships, is there a gap between the response you want and the response you're getting? If so, what could be causing these gaps?

15. How might "easing up" your focus on these people change your and their responses? To consider this question, complete the following statements:

I could hold these people less tightly by . . .

By easing up, I might change my attitude to . . .

By easing up, their response might change to . . .

If I stop clinging, the risks would be . . .

16. a. Are you willing to take the risk of easing up or letting go? Explain.

    b. What might happen if you don't?

17. Often jealousy and many of its accompanying attitudes and actions are sin. What might you need to repent of to overcome your jealousy? ■

NOTE
  1. James Dobson, *Love Must Be Tough* (Irving, TX: Word Publishers, 1983), pages 176-177.

Is Her Life Really Better?

Questions for your small group.

LESSON ONE

1. Do you think Christians avoid applying the word *greed* to themselves? Why, or why not?
2. To camouflage our attitudes, what other words might we use for *greed*?
3. Is greed confined to money and material possessions? Explain.
4. How is greed acceptable in our culture?
5. Would the meaning of *greed* change from culture to culture? Why, or why not?
6. Can a person be wealthy and still be close to God? Why, or why not?
7. Do you believe God promises prosperity to all of His children? Explain.
8. How are greed and envy related? Is it a cause-and-effect relationship? Support your answer.

9. Why could stewardship be a difficult concept to grasp?
10. In light of stewardship, how should Christians treat each other?

LESSON TWO

1. Do we usually recognize the envy in our lives? Why, or why not?
2. How can we become aware of our envy?
3. How can we discover the root cause(s) of our envy?
4. How do envy and covetousness affect our relationships?
5. Are there any times when coveting would be a good attitude?
6. Do you believe that self-image is tied to envy and coveting? If so, how?
7. Do you find it difficult to relate to and/or love others who have more than you do? Explain.
8. How does our envy express itself in words and actions?
9. How does it feel to be the target of someone's envy?
10. Can a relationship survive envy? Why, or why not?

LESSON THREE

1. How did comparison and competition play a role in Adam and Eve's fall as described in Genesis 3?
2. When are we most tempted to compare and compete?

3. How can we cause other people to compare and compete with us?
4. How do comparison and competition relate to the pursuit of excellence?
5. How can we tell if we are competitive in a destructive way?
6. Why do some people always seem to want to be "right" or "the best?"
7. Can comparison be spiritually motivating in a healthy way? If so, how?
8. How can comparison and competitiveness destroy a group?
9. How can we monitor our inner attitudes so as not to destroy relationships with comparisons?
10. How do we compete with ourselves? What are the results?

LESSON FOUR

1. Do you think jealousy is an instinctive or a learned response? Explain.
2. Is jealousy always related to loss? Why, or why not?
3. What are the attributes of healthy and unhealthy jealousy? Compare and contrast them.
4. Of whom are you most apt to be jealous? Why?
5. Compare envy and jealousy. Is one more destructive than the other? Explain.
6. How is God's jealousy different from ours?
7. Is jealousy always evident? Why, or why not?

8. Whom does unhealthy jealousy hurt the most?
9. How does jealousy deflect our own shortcomings?
10. What personal responsibility is necessary to overcome jealousy? ∎

BIBLIOGRAPHY

Becoming
the Real You

Books for study and growth.

Chisholm, Gloria. *When You Can't Get Along.*
Colorado Springs, CO: NavPress, 1990.

Couchman, Judith. *Getting a Grip on Guilt.*
Colorado Springs, CO: NavPress, 1990.

Couchman, Judith. *If I'm So Good, Why Don't
I Act That Way?* Colorado Springs, CO:
NavPress, 1991.

Friday, Nancy. *Jealousy.* New York: Bantam
Books, 1985.

Hancock, Maxine. *Living on Less and Liking
It More.* Chicago, IL: Moody Press, 1976.

Hilt, James. *How to Have a Better Relationship With Anybody: A Biblical Approach.*
Chicago, IL: Moody Press, 1984.

Lerner, Harriet Goldhor, Ph.D. *The Dance of Anger.* New York: Harper & Row, Publishers, 1985.

McGinnis, Alan Loy. *The Friendship Factor.* Minneapolis, MN: Augsburg Publishing House, 1979. ∎

A U T H O R

Judith Couchman serves as Director of
Communications for The Navigators and
also develops new products for NavPress.
She is the former editor of *Sunday Digest*
and *Christian Life,* and has worked as a
public relations professional and a journalism
teacher. She has also taught writing at con-
ferences around the United States.

Judith has published many times in
magazines and curriculum publications.
In addition to this study book, she's also
published *Getting a Grip on Guilt* and *If
I'm So Good, Why Don't I Act That Way?*
(NavPress).

Judith has received top awards from
the Evangelical Press Association, the
International Association of Business Com-
municators, the Advertising Federation, and
several high school press associations (for her

teaching). She's also listed in *Who's Who of Female Executives.*

She holds a B.S. in education and an M.A. in journalism, collects art by "people who aren't famous yet," and lives in Colorado Springs, Colorado. ■

OTHER TITLES IN THIS SERIES

Additional *CRISISPOINTS* Bible studies
include:

> *Getting a Grip on Guilt* by Judith
> Couchman. Learn to live a life free
> from guilt.

> *Nobody's Perfect, So Why Do I Try to Be?*
> by Nancy Groom. Get over the need to do
> everything right.

> *So What If You've Failed?* by Penelope J.
> Stokes. Use your mistakes to become a
> more loving, godly woman.

> *When You Can't Get Along* by Gloria
> Chisholm. How to resolve conflict
> according to the Bible.

When Your Marriage Disappoints You
by Janet Chester Bly. Hope and help for
improving your marriage.

Where Is God When I Need Him Most? by
Janet Kobobel. Find God's comfort when
it feels like He's abandoned you.

You're Better Than You Think! by
Madalene Harris. How to overcome
shame and develop a healthy self-image.

These studies can be purchased at a Christian bookstore. Or order a catalog from
NavPress, Customer Services, P. O. Box
35001, Colorado Springs, CO 80935. Or call
1-800-366-7788 for information. ■